CRAFTY
IDEAS FOR
PRESENTS

For Natasha Ilana

First published in Great Britain in 1990 by
**Exley Publications Ltd, 16 Chalk Hill,
Watford, Herts WD1 4BN, United Kingdom.**

Second printing, 1990

Text copyright © Myrna Daitz 1990
Illustrations copyright © Gillian Chapman 1990

British Library Cataloguing in Publication Data
Daitz, Myrna.
    Crafty ideas for presents.
    1. Gifts, making.
    I.   Title.
    II. Gillian Chapman.
    745.5

ISBN 1-85015-156-3

Series designers: Gillian Chapman and
Linda Sullivan.
Editorial: Margaret Montgomery.
Typeset by Brush Off Studios, St Albans,
Herts AL3 4PH.
Printed and bound in Hungary.

CRAFTY
IDEAS FOR
PRESENTS

Myrna Daitz

Pictures
by
Gillian Chapman

▤EXLEY

Contents

Introduction

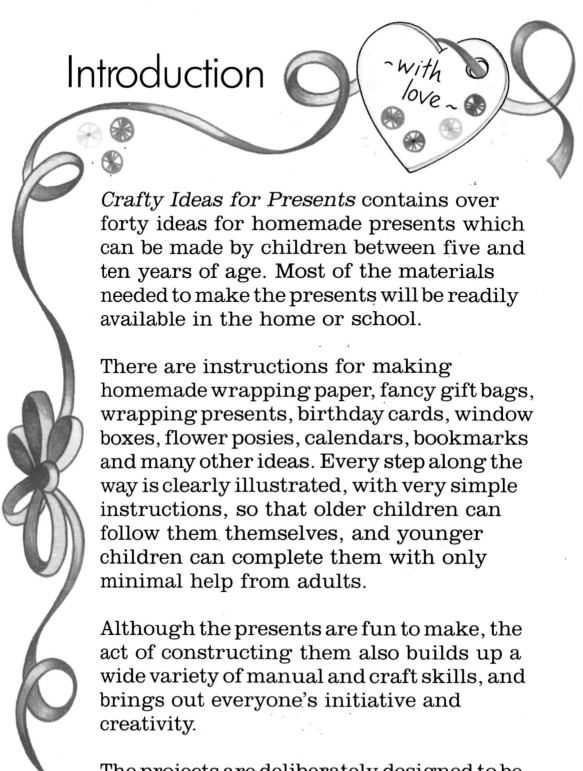

Crafty Ideas for Presents contains over forty ideas for homemade presents which can be made by children between five and ten years of age. Most of the materials needed to make the presents will be readily available in the home or school.

There are instructions for making homemade wrapping paper, fancy gift bags, wrapping presents, birthday cards, window boxes, flower posies, calendars, bookmarks and many other ideas. Every step along the way is clearly illustrated, with very simple instructions, so that older children can follow them themselves, and younger children can complete them with only minimal help from adults.

Although the presents are fun to make, the act of constructing them also builds up a wide variety of manual and craft skills, and brings out everyone's initiative and creativity.

The projects are deliberately designed to be easy. There is nothing worse than starting a project that is too difficult to complete. Everyone's first experience of crafting should bring a feeling of achievement and creation. Myrna Daitz, the author, is a schoolteacher herself, with years of experience of craft teaching. She has called upon teacher friends to help with ideas and to make sure that every project has been well tested.

Don't worry if some of the results don't look at all like the illustrations in the book. It doesn't matter! It is much more important that everyone feels free to be creative and enjoys themselves. The real achievement lies not in copying the ideas in the book: it comes from making the most of the materials you have to hand, and being as inventive as you can with the basic ideas we have given you.

Learn lots – and enjoy yourself!

Printed Wrapping Paper

1. Make sure the tile you choose has a deeply-embossed pattern on it.

2. Thickly paint all over the tile.

3. Lay the white paper over the tile then roll it with the old rolling pin.

4. Repaint the tile then repeat the rolling until all the paper is completely covered on one side only with an interesting pattern.

5. Leave to dry then use it to wrap your home-made presents.

Parent's Handy Hints :-
As wrapping paper is very expensive, you will find this a good cheap alternative.
The tiles can be washed and used again.

Fancy Gift Bags

1. Cut out two rectangular pieces of paper both the same size.

2. Decorate the paper with the felt tipped pens.

What you need :–

A piece of plain paper.
Strong glue.
Ribbon or tape.
A Stapler.
Felt-tipped pens.

3. Glue the sides and bottom edges of the paper together.

4. Make two handles from the strip of cardboard. Staple them to the top of the gift bag.

Parent's Handy Hints :–
You can make pretty gift tags to match the gift bags.
LOOK OUT for more tag ideas throughout this book!

Wrapping a Present

What you need :—

Wrapping paper
(see "Printed Wrapping
Paper" ideas on p.10)
Scissors.
Adhesive tape.
Ribbon or tape.
A stapler.

1. Lay the paper very flat on a table.

2. Put the present in the middle of the paper. If the paper is too big, trim the edges so that it is easier to fold.

Make Christmas presents into "crackers" & use tinsel, glitter and foil to decorate them.

3. Fold the two long sides over the top of the present and turn in the two ends to form a point.

4. Fold the pointed flaps over the top of the parcel. Put a small piece of tape on the flaps to stop them from opening.

5. Tie the parcel ribbon tightly around the parcel using tiny pieces of tape to hold it in place. Finish with a big bow at the top.

Pretty bows can be made from tape or ribbon by winding them into loops and securing with a staple.

Clown Card

What you need :-
White cardboard.
Small piece of felt.
Glue.
Scissors.
Felt pens or crayons.
A handkerchief.

1. Fold the cardboard in half.

2. Draw a funny clown on the front and decorate with felt tipped pens or crayons.

3. To make the pocket, cut out a 5cm (2″) square of felt. Glue around three sides, leaving the top open, and stick on to the clown's tummy.

4. When the glue is dry, put the handkerchief in the pocket. Don't forget to write your message inside the card.

Parent's Handy Hint:-

Another idea would be to use a red felt heart as the pocket & tuck a pretty handkerchief in the top.

Father's Card

21cm. (8")

17cm. (6½")

1. Take a piece of cardboard approximately 21cm x 17cm (8" x 6½") and fold it in half.

2. Look through old mail order books to find pictures of items suitable for Father.

3/4. Cut the pictures out carefully and glue them on to the front of the card.

5. Write your message on the front and inside with a felt tipped pen.

Parent's Handy Hint :-
An easy-to-make card which can be adapted to suit anyone by the choice of cut-outs.

To Father

Heart Card

What you need :—
Cardboard, approx. 21cm. x 17cm. (8½" x 6½")

Red gummed paper.
A pencil & felt pen.
Scissors.
Tissue paper.
Glue.

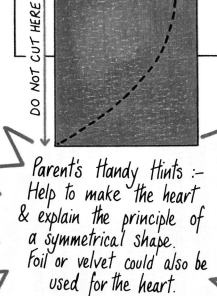

DO NOT CUT HERE

1. Take a piece of cardboard approximately 21cm x 17cm (8½" x 6"). Fold it in half and write a message inside.

2. Now fold a piece of gummed paper in half. Draw half a heart shape up to the left-hand folded edge.

3. From the folded edge cut out the heart shape from both pieces of paper leaving the folded edge uncut.

4. Unfold the heart. You now have a symmetrical heart shape. Glue the heart to the front of the card.

5. Crumple up small pieces of tissue paper to make balls.

6. Glue the balls around the edge of the heart shape and write a greeting on the front.

Parent's Handy Hints :—
Help to make the heart & explain the principle of a symmetrical shape.
Foil or velvet could also be used for the heart.

I love You

Bell Card

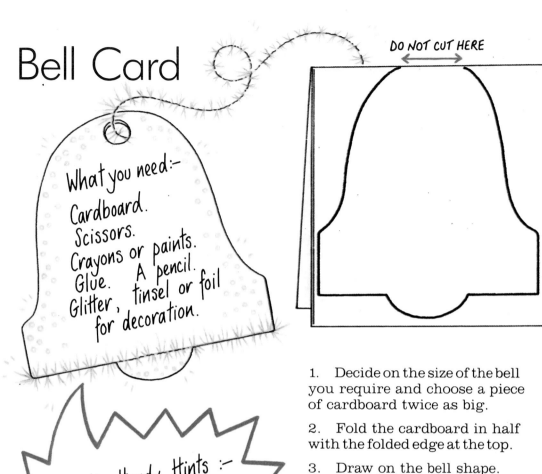

DO NOT CUT HERE

What you need:-
Cardboard.
Scissors.
Crayons or paints.
Glue. A pencil.
Glitter, tinsel or foil
for decoration.

Parent's Handy Hints :-
Make sure the top folded edge is not cut.
Different sized bells can be used as Christmas tree decorations or parcel tags.

1. Decide on the size of the bell you require and choose a piece of cardboard twice as big.

2. Fold the cardboard in half with the folded edge at the top.

3. Draw on the bell shape.

4. Cut out the shape from both pieces of cardboard, taking care *not* to cut the top folded edge.

5. Decorate your bell with crayons or paints, or glue on silver or gold glitter, tinsel or silver foil.

17

Egg-shaped Card

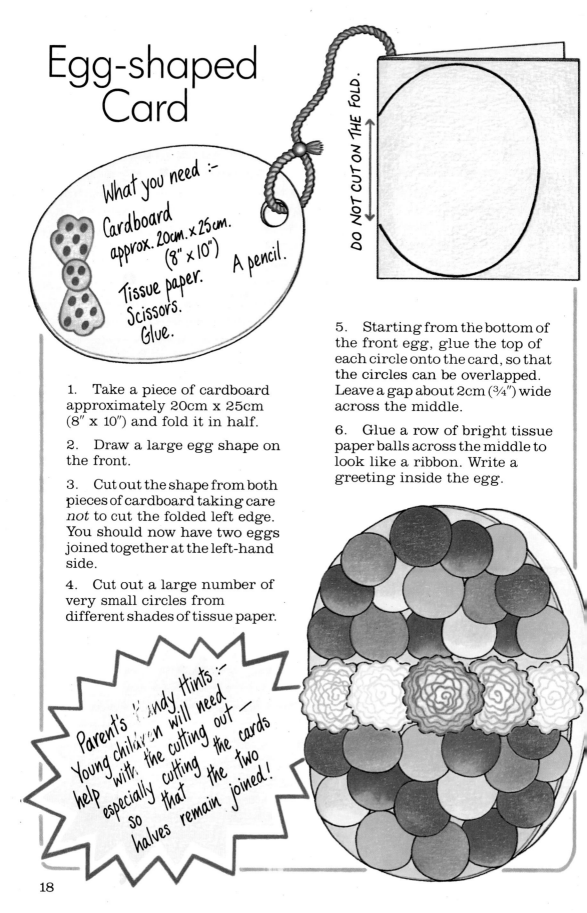

What you need :-
Cardboard approx. 20cm. x 25cm. (8" x 10")
Tissue paper.
Scissors.
Glue.
A pencil.

1. Take a piece of cardboard approximately 20cm x 25cm (8" x 10") and fold it in half.

2. Draw a large egg shape on the front.

3. Cut out the shape from both pieces of cardboard taking care *not* to cut the folded left edge. You should now have two eggs joined together at the left-hand side.

4. Cut out a large number of very small circles from different shades of tissue paper.

5. Starting from the bottom of the front egg, glue the top of each circle onto the card, so that the circles can be overlapped. Leave a gap about 2cm (¾") wide across the middle.

6. Glue a row of bright tissue paper balls across the middle to look like a ribbon. Write a greeting inside the egg.

Parent's Handy Hints :-
Young children will need help with the cutting out — especially cutting the cards so that the two halves remain joined!

18

Fluffy Cards

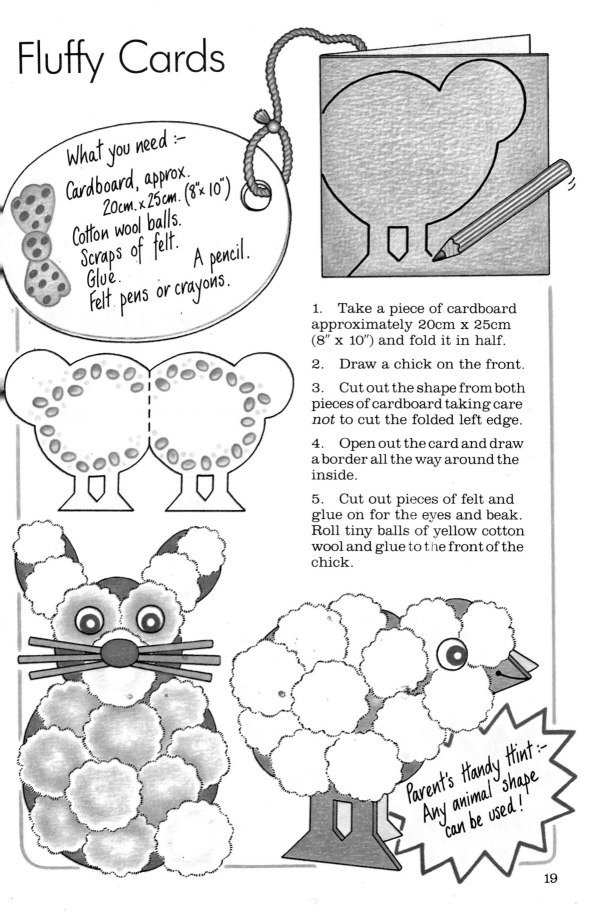

What you need :-

Cardboard, approx.
20cm. x 25cm. (8" x 10")
Cotton wool balls.
Scraps of felt.   A pencil.
Glue.
Felt pens or crayons.

1.   Take a piece of cardboard approximately 20cm x 25cm (8" x 10") and fold it in half.

2.   Draw a chick on the front.

3.   Cut out the shape from both pieces of cardboard taking care *not* to cut the folded left edge.

4.   Open out the card and draw a border all the way around the inside.

5.   Cut out pieces of felt and glue on for the eyes and beak. Roll tiny balls of yellow cotton wool and glue to the front of the chick.

Parent's Handy Hint :-
Any animal shape can be used!

19

Standing Christmas Tree

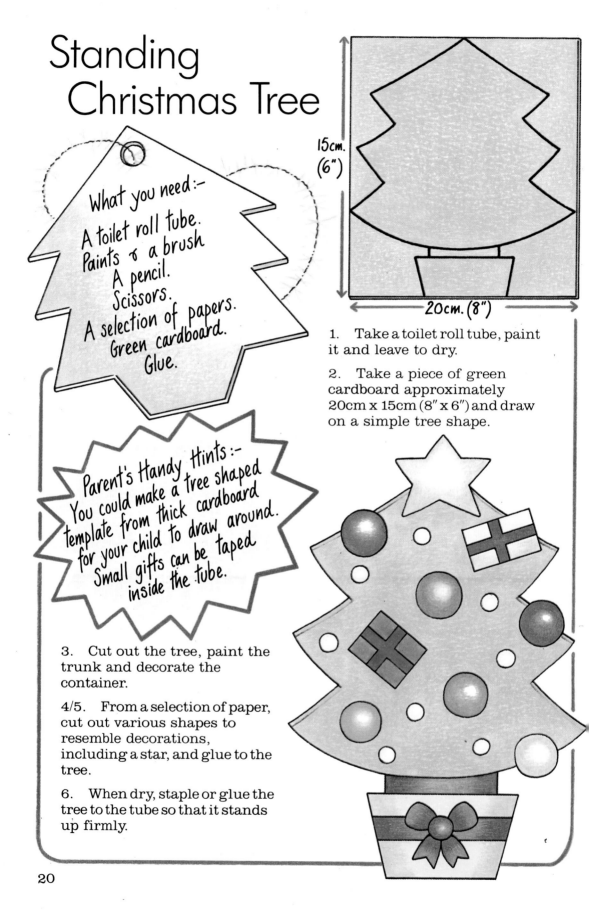

15cm. (6")

20cm. (8")

What you need :-

A toilet roll tube.
Paints & a brush
A pencil.
Scissors.
A selection of papers.
Green cardboard.
Glue.

1.　Take a toilet roll tube, paint it and leave to dry.

2.　Take a piece of green cardboard approximately 20cm x 15cm (8" x 6") and draw on a simple tree shape.

Parent's Handy Hints :-

You could make a tree shaped template from thick cardboard for your child to draw around. Small gifts can be taped inside the tube.

3.　Cut out the tree, paint the trunk and decorate the container.

4/5.　From a selection of paper, cut out various shapes to resemble decorations, including a star, and glue to the tree.

6.　When dry, staple or glue the tree to the tube so that it stands up firmly.

Christmas Angel

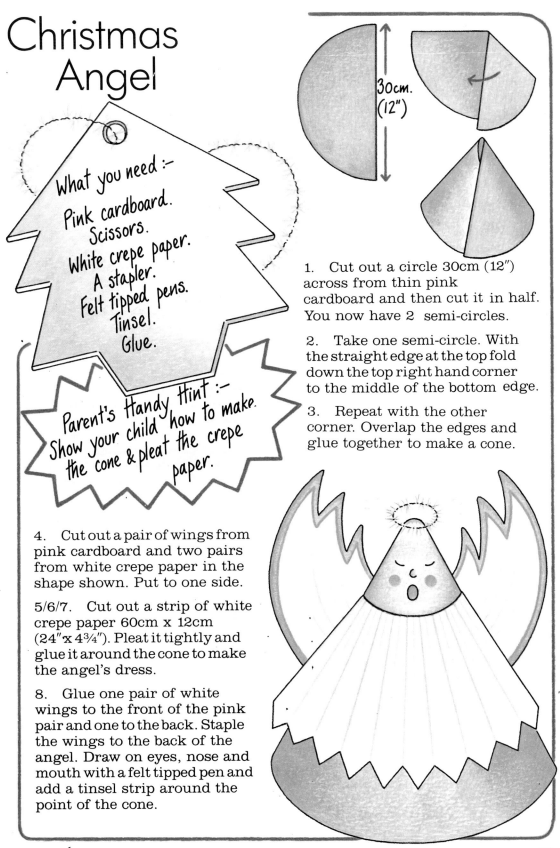

What you need :-

Pink cardboard.
Scissors.
White crepe paper.
A stapler.
Felt tipped pens.
Tinsel.
Glue.

Parent's Handy Hint :-
Show your child how to make the cone & pleat the crepe paper.

1. Cut out a circle 30cm (12″) across from thin pink cardboard and then cut it in half. You now have 2 semi-circles.

2. Take one semi-circle. With the straight edge at the top fold down the top right hand corner to the middle of the bottom edge.

3. Repeat with the other corner. Overlap the edges and glue together to make a cone.

4. Cut out a pair of wings from pink cardboard and two pairs from white crepe paper in the shape shown. Put to one side.

5/6/7. Cut out a strip of white crepe paper 60cm x 12cm (24″ x 4¾″). Pleat it tightly and glue it around the cone to make the angel's dress.

8. Glue one pair of white wings to the front of the pink pair and one to the back. Staple the wings to the back of the angel. Draw on eyes, nose and mouth with a felt tipped pen and add a tinsel strip around the point of the cone.

A Bon-Bon Basket

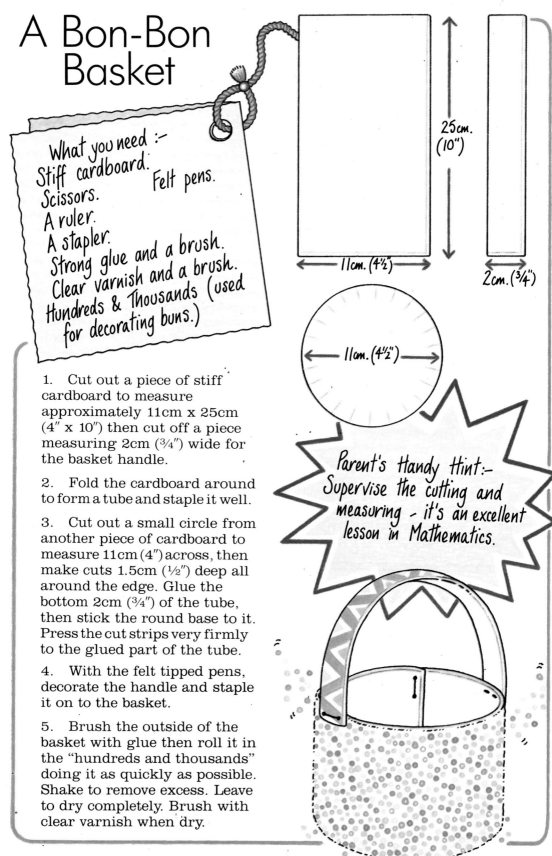

What you need :-
Stiff cardboard.
Felt pens.
Scissors.
A ruler.
A stapler.
Strong glue and a brush.
Clear varnish and a brush.
Hundreds & Thousands (used for decorating buns.)

25cm. (10")

11cm. (4½")

2cm. (¾")

11cm. (4½")

1.   Cut out a piece of stiff cardboard to measure approximately 11cm x 25cm (4" x 10") then cut off a piece measuring 2cm (¾") wide for the basket handle.

2.   Fold the cardboard around to form a tube and staple it well.

3.   Cut out a small circle from another piece of cardboard to measure 11cm (4") across, then make cuts 1.5cm (½") deep all around the edge. Glue the bottom 2cm (¾") of the tube, then stick the round base to it. Press the cut strips very firmly to the glued part of the tube.

4.   With the felt tipped pens, decorate the handle and staple it on to the basket.

5.   Brush the outside of the basket with glue then roll it in the "hundreds and thousands" doing it as quickly as possible. Shake to remove excess. Leave to dry completely. Brush with clear varnish when dry.

Parent's Handy Hint:-
Supervise the cutting and measuring - it's an excellent lesson in Mathematics.

Sweetie Gift Box

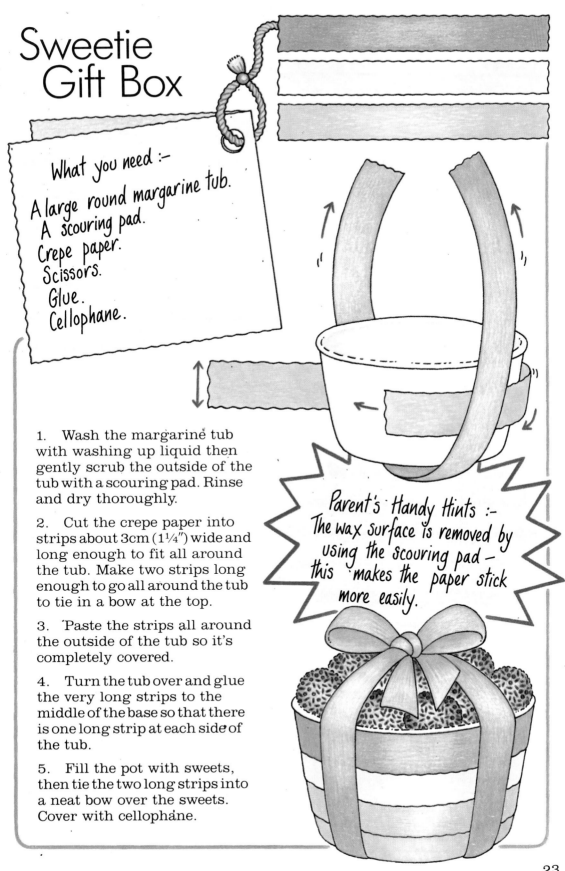

What you need :-

A large round margarine tub.
A scouring pad.
Crepe paper.
Scissors.
Glue.
Cellophane.

1. Wash the margarine tub with washing up liquid then gently scrub the outside of the tub with a scouring pad. Rinse and dry thoroughly.

2. Cut the crepe paper into strips about 3cm (1¼") wide and long enough to fit all around the tub. Make two strips long enough to go all around the tub to tie in a bow at the top.

3. Paste the strips all around the outside of the tub so it's completely covered.

4. Turn the tub over and glue the very long strips to the middle of the base so that there is one long strip at each side of the tub.

5. Fill the pot with sweets, then tie the two long strips into a neat bow over the sweets. Cover with cellophane.

Parent's Handy Hints :-
The wax surface is removed by using the scouring pad – this makes the paper stick more easily.

Coconut Snowballs

What you need :-
55g. (2oz.) shredded coconut.
55g. (2oz.) plain biscuits (crackers).
55g. (2oz.) sultanas.
55g. (2oz.) almonds.
75g. (2½ fl. oz.) fresh cream.
A rolling pin.   A knife.
A basin.   A spoon.
A bag.

1.   Crumble the biscuits (crackers) with a rolling-pin.

2.   Chop the nuts and the fruit into small pieces.

3.   Put the crumbs, chopped nuts and fruit into a basin and add the cream.

4.   Mix well.

5.   Shape the mixture into small balls.

6.   Put the coconut into a bag and drop the balls in, a few at a time.

7.   Roll them about and shake them in the bag. This helps to make them rounder.

Parent's Handy Hint :-
You can make snowmen by putting two coconut balls together. Use pieces of currant and cherry for the eyes & mouth.

8.   When you take them out, they should be covered in coconut. They are ready to eat straightaway.

Crispy Crispies

Supervise the melting of the chocolate!

What you need :-
Cornflakes or rice crispies.
Bar of chocolate.
125g. (4oz.) icing (confectioner's) sugar.
Paper cases.
1-2 tablespoons hot water.
Chopped cherry & angelica.
A bowl of hot water.
A bowl & a spoon.

1. Put the chocolate in the basin and place it over a bowl of hot, but *not* boiling, water until the chocolate melts.

2. Remove the basin from the bowl and stir in the cereal, being sure it's well mixed in and all covered in chocolate.

3. Wash your hands. Now for the messy part. With your hands, roll the crispies into small balls. Put into paper cases and leave to set.

4. Mix the sugar and hot water together in a basin until smooth. Put half a teaspoon on top of each crispie.

5. Decorate the top of each crispie with a piece of cherry and two pieces of angelica.

Gingerbread Men

What you need :–
85g. (3½ oz.) margarine.
2 tablespoons of Golden Syrup.
57g. (2oz.) sugar.
½ teaspoon of bicarbonate
        of soda.
200g. (8oz.) flour.
1½ teaspoons of ground ginger.
Currants or raisins.
A long handled wooden spoon.
A sieve.   A rolling pin.

1.   Trace our picture of a gingerbread man then transfer it to a piece of thick cardboard and cut it out.

2.   In a pan, heat the margarine with the golden syrup and the sugar. Do not allow to boil.

3.   Dissolve the bicarbonate of soda in a little water and add this to the syrup mixture. Stir gently with the wooden spoon.

4.   Remove the pan from the cooker and stand on a heat-proof surface.

Parent's Handy Hints :–
Talk to your child about
SAFETY in the KITCHEN.
The melting of the syrup &
sugar, and the use of the
oven MUST BE
        SUPERVISED.

5. Put the sieve over the pan and gently add the flour and ground ginger, shaking them through the sieve. Mix well to make a firm dough. Put the mixture in a clean, dry bowl and cover with a tea cloth. Leave for one hour.

6. Roll out the dough then make the gingerbread men by gently placing your shape on the dough and cutting around it. Use the currants for eyes and nose.

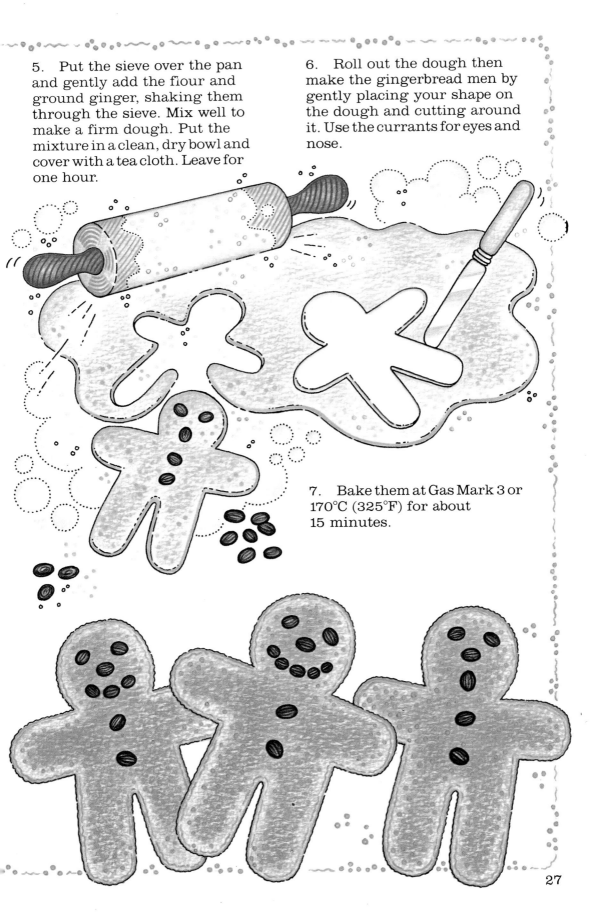

7. Bake them at Gas Mark 3 or 170°C (325°F) for about 15 minutes.

Chocolate Truffles

What you need :-
Small paper cases.
110g. (4oz.) icing sugar (confectioner's sugar)
85g. (2½ oz.) cocoa powder.
3 tablespoons of thick cream.
Chocolate vermicelli.
A large bowl.   A sieve.
A wooden spoon.

1. Put the sieve over the bowl and shake the sugar and cocoa into the bowl through it.

2. Gently mix in the cream.

3. Thoroughly dust your hands with sugar and roll the mixture into small balls.

4. Roll each ball in chocolate vermicelli.

5. Leave for 2 hours in the refrigerator.

6. Put the truffles in the paper cases and put into a decorated container. DELIVER THE PRESENT IMMEDIATELY.

Adult's Handy Hint :-
If the present is for an adult, add a few drops of rum to the cream!

Date Surprises

What you need :-
Fresh dates.
Whole skinned almonds.
Powdered cardamon seeds.
Marzipan.
A sharp knife.

Parent's Handy Hint :- DO NOT let the child use the sharp knife without ADULT SUPERVISION.

1. Slit the dates with a sharp-pointed knife and remove the stones.

2. Sprinkle some cardamon powder inside the date and put in an almond. Close the date.

3. Cut out a small square of marzipan and seal the date inside the marzipan.

Look out for the Sweet Gift Box ideas on pages 22 - 23 !

29

Window Box

What you need:-
A cereal box.
Scissors.
Brown paint & a brush.
Gummed paper or wall paper.
Bright tissue paper.
Glue.
Cardboard.

8cm.
(3")

FLOWER SHAPE.

LEAF SHAPE.

1.　Take a breakfast cereal box and cut across to leave a base 8cm (3") high.

2.　Paint the inside brown to look like soil.

3.　Cover the outside with gummed paper or wallpaper.

4.　Cut out this flower shape several times from bright tissue paper.

5.　Cut out this leaf shape several times from green tissue paper.

6. Take a piece of green tissue paper 14cm x 9cm (6" x 4"). Roll up and glue the long edge to make a stalk. Glue the flowers around the stalk and add the leaves.

7. Cut out a strip of cardboard 2cm (¾") deep and 3cm (1¼") longer than the box. Fold over 1.5cm (⅝") at each end. Glue the flowers to the cardboard strip. Glue the folded ends of the strip firmly to the inside of the box so that the stalks rest on the bottom.

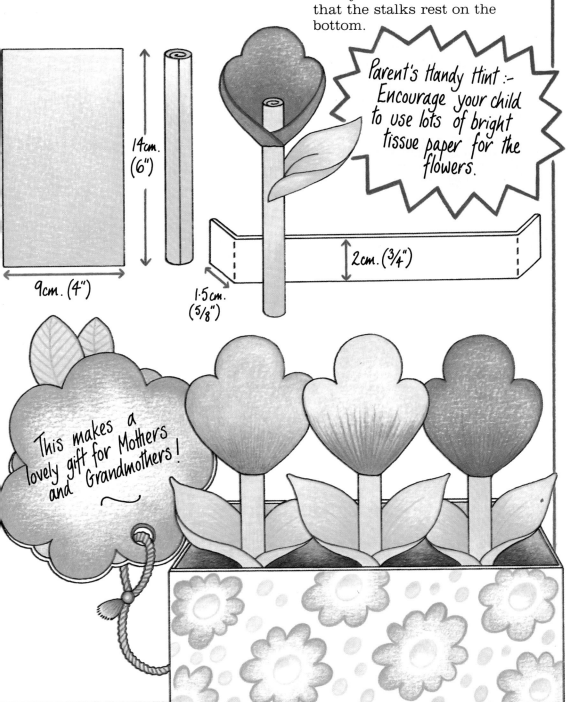

14cm. (6")

9cm. (4")

1·5cm. (5/8")

2cm. (¾")

Parent's Handy Hint :- Encourage your child to use lots of bright tissue paper for the flowers.

This makes a lovely gift for Mothers and Grandmothers!

A Thirsty Flower Posy

What you need :-
A bunch of white flowers (carnations, white pinks or daisies) Tall glasses. Ribbon. 3 bottles of food dye. Large piece of silver foil.

1. Put cold water in each of the three glasses. Add food dye to each glass. Use quite a lot to make very deep shades.

2. Stand the flowers in the water. Leave for a few hours in a cool room.

3. When the petals have taken up some of the dye from the water, dry the stems gently on absorbent paper. Wrap the bouquet up in silver foil and tie with a big bow. Deliver your present immediately.

Parent's Handy Hints :- It is very interesting to see how the stems absorb the dye and to see the dye at the edges of the petals.

It proves to children that flowers "drink" water!

Paper Plate Flowers

1. Make flower designs on the plates using your felt tipped pens.

2. Some of the plates can be cut into petal shapes, others left as they are.

3. Make the middles of the flowers from the small paper cases. Paint them first and then glue them to the middle of the flower.

4. Glue or staple the drinking straws to the back of the flower.

5. Make leaves from the thick paper and paint them green. Glue or staple them to the stem.

Adult's Handy Hint :-
Encourage your child to copy real flower shapes from gardening books!

Pom-pom Presents

10cm. (4")

4cm. (1½")

1. Cut out two circles from the cardboard about 10cm (4") across.

2. Now cut out a smaller circle, measuring about 4cm (1½") across, from the middle of each of these. You now have two large rings.

3. Hold both cardboard rings together and wind the wool around. Keep doing this until there is hardly any room in the middle. Use the darning needle when it gets too hard to thread the wool with your fingers.

4. When you have finished, cut the wool all around the edges, cutting between the two rings.

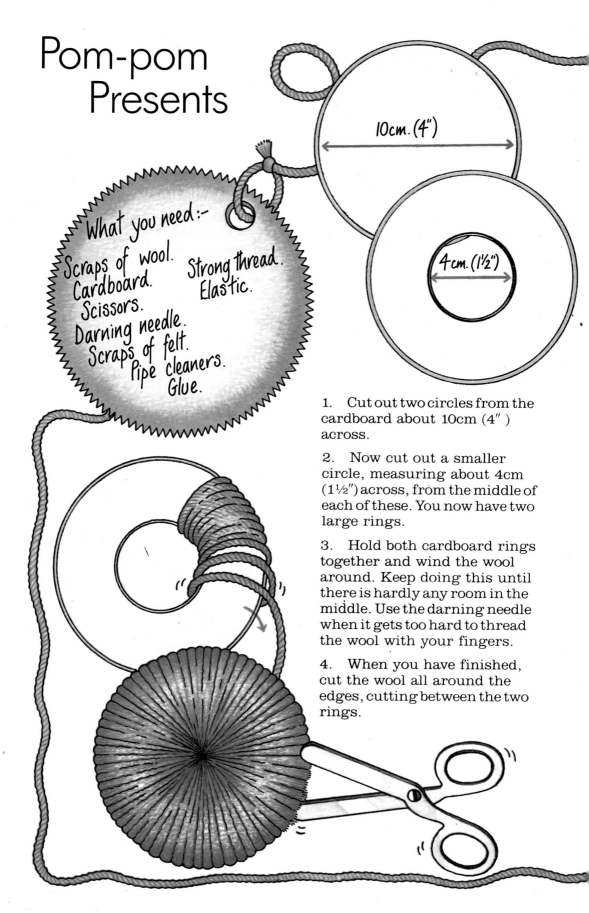

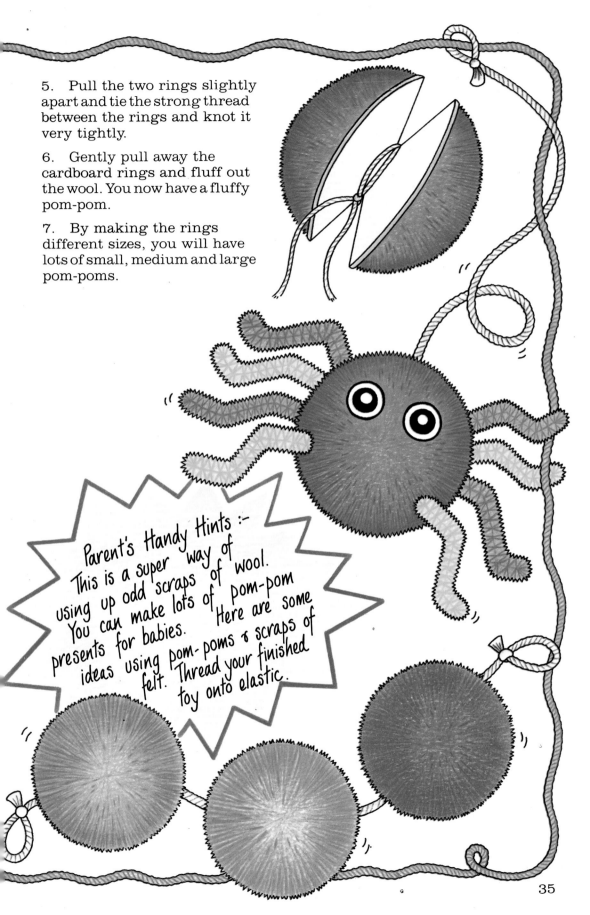

5. Pull the two rings slightly apart and tie the strong thread between the rings and knot it very tightly.

6. Gently pull away the cardboard rings and fluff out the wool. You now have a fluffy pom-pom.

7. By making the rings different sizes, you will have lots of small, medium and large pom-poms.

Parent's Handy Hints :-
This is a super way of using up odd scraps of wool. You can make lots of pom-pom presents for babies. Here are some ideas using pom-poms & scraps of felt. Thread your finished toy onto elastic.

A Photographmobile

1.   Completely cover the coat hanger with silver foil and tinsel.

2.   Cut out six pieces of cardboard, each one just slightly bigger than the photographs. Make some round, some square, and some star shaped.

3.   Glue the photographs on to the middle of the cardboard leaving a border showing around each one.

4.   Make a small hole at the top of each piece of cardboard and put a long piece of thread through it from the back. When it is long enough, make a knot in the thread to stop it slipping through the cardboard.

5.   Tie the thread to the bottom of the coat hanger. Make the thread different sizes for each photograph.

Adult's Handy Hint :-
Both these projects make lovely presents for grand parents !

36

Remember Me Calendar

What you need :-
A piece of cardboard 25cm. x 19cm.
(10" x 7½").
White paper.
Cord or tape.
Glue.
A large photograph of yourself
or a special pet.
Small calendar.
Finger paints.

1.   Cut the cardboard to measure approximately 25cm long and 19cm wide (10" x 7½").

2.   Cut the white paper to cover the cardboard and glue it on.

3.   Carefully glue the photograph to fit the middle of the white paper.

4.   Make a loop from the cord and glue or staple to the top to make a hanger for the calendar.

5.   Glue the calendar dates pad under the photograph, and decorate the frame with finger paints.

CALENDAR.

Multi-shape Clown

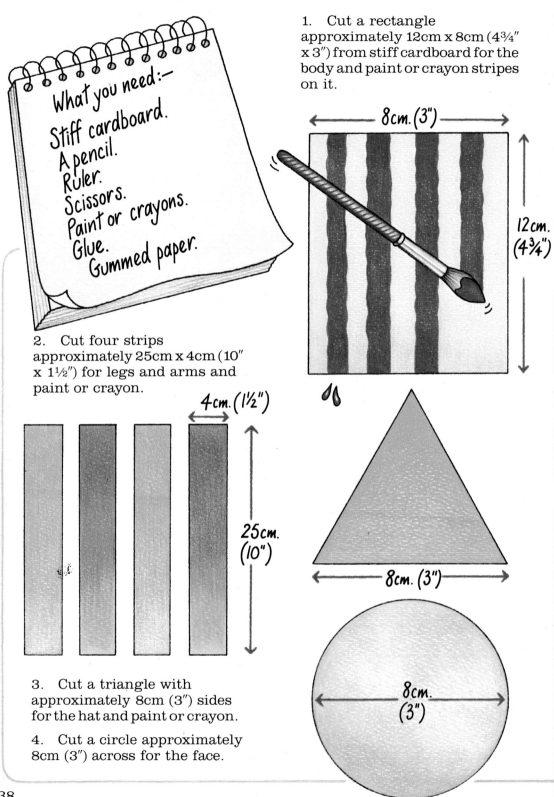

1. Cut a rectangle approximately 12cm x 8cm (4¾" x 3") from stiff cardboard for the body and paint or crayon stripes on it.

What you need:-
Stiff cardboard.
A pencil.
Ruler.
Scissors.
Paint or crayons.
Glue.
Gummed paper.

8cm. (3")

12cm. (4¾")

2. Cut four strips approximately 25cm x 4cm (10" x 1½") for legs and arms and paint or crayon.

4cm. (1½")

25cm. (10")

8cm. (3")

3. Cut a triangle with approximately 8cm (3") sides for the hat and paint or crayon.

4. Cut a circle approximately 8cm (3") across for the face.

8cm. (3")

5. Fold the legs and arms in a concertina fashion and glue or staple to the body.

6. Draw and paint the face, or use gummed paper for the features. Glue on the hat.

7. To make buttons, cut circles out of bright paper and glue to body.

Parent's Handy Hints:—
The clown can be produced in any size and used as a hanging mobile by attaching a thread to the hat. While constructing the clown the child will assimilate shape and size, and gain a good knowledge of measurement.

Dotty Door Dog

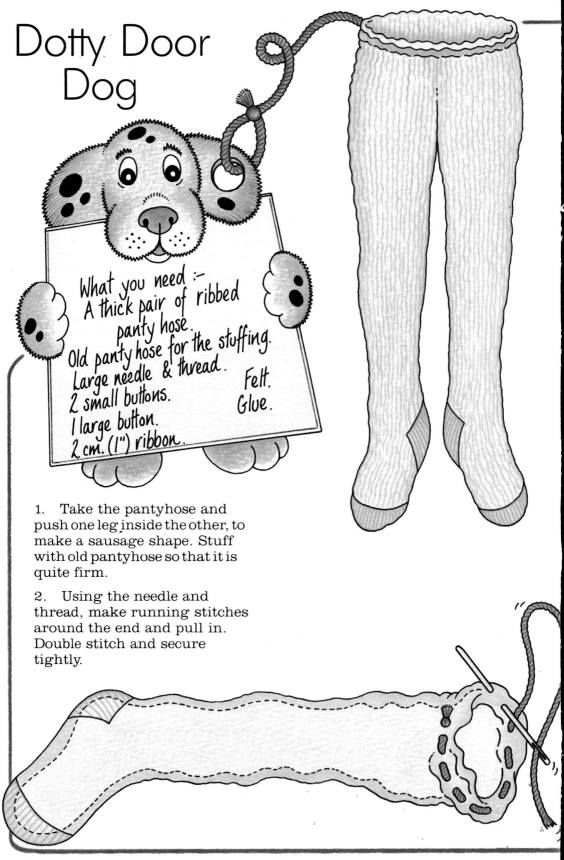

What you need :-
A thick pair of ribbed panty hose.
Old panty hose for the stuffing.
Large needle & thread.
2 small buttons.
1 large button.
2 cm. (1") ribbon.
Felt.
Glue.

1. Take the pantyhose and push one leg inside the other, to make a sausage shape. Stuff with old pantyhose so that it is quite firm.

2. Using the needle and thread, make running stitches around the end and pull in. Double stitch and secure tightly.

3. Tie a length of ribbon around the ankle of the pantyhose to make the neck.

4. Cut out six oval-shape pieces of felt – four for the legs and two for the ears – and a piece 3cm x 15cm (6″ x 1¼″) for the tail. Stitch them onto the body. Cut out felt spots and glue them to the body.

3 cm. (1¼″)

15cm. (6″)

5. Sew on the large button for the nose and the two smaller ones for the eyes.

Parent's Handy Hints :–
If your child is not ready for sewing, an adult could help, or strong glue could be used instead to attach the felt & buttons.

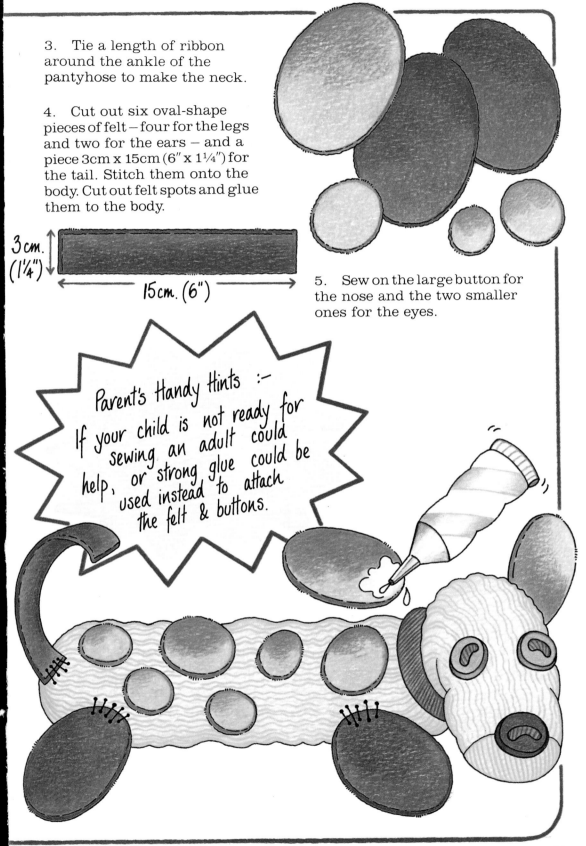

41

A Button and String Picture

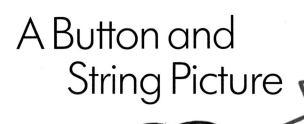

Adult's Handy Hint :-

Sorting the buttons into different shades and sizes is an excellent Mathematical learning experience!

What you need :-

A piece of thick cardboard.
A ball of string.
A pencil.
Scissors.
Glue.
Old buttons.

1. Using the pencil, draw a tortoise on the cardboard.

Look out for a picture of a tortoise in a book that you can copy, or use this shape.

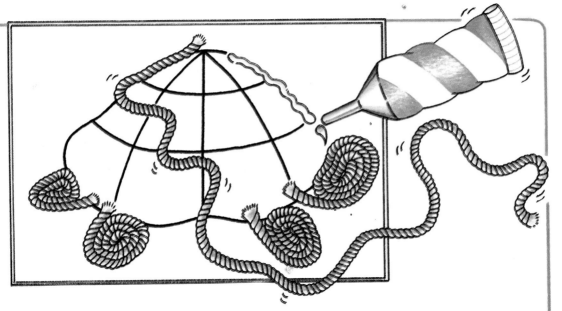

2. Go over the pencil lines with glue, then carefully press the string along the lines, winding it around to make the head, feet and tail. Criss-cross the string from side to side to make the shell pattern.

3. Glue a button on the head for an eye, then buttons in each section of the shell.

4. To hang the picture, make a loop from a piece of string and glue or staple to the top.

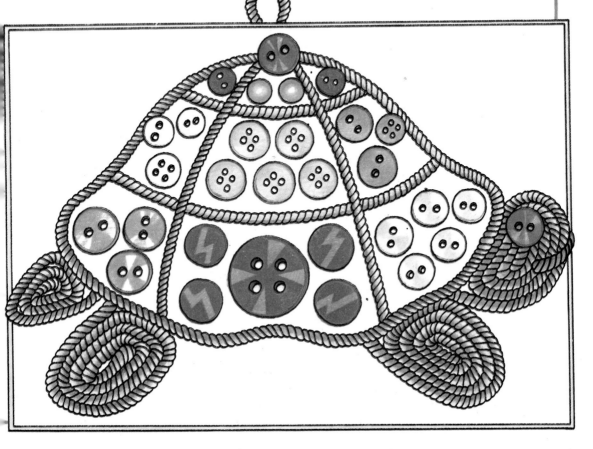

Stamps Bookmark

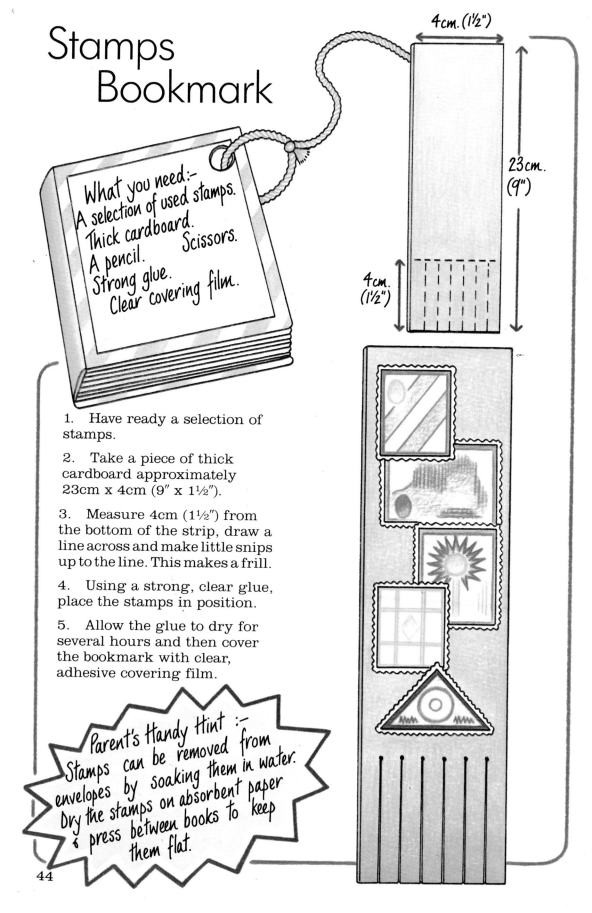

What you need:-
A selection of used stamps.
Thick cardboard.
A pencil.   Scissors.
Strong glue.
Clear covering film.

1.   Have ready a selection of stamps.

2.   Take a piece of thick cardboard approximately 23cm x 4cm (9" x 1½").

3.   Measure 4cm (1½") from the bottom of the strip, draw a line across and make little snips up to the line. This makes a frill.

4.   Using a strong, clear glue, place the stamps in position.

5.   Allow the glue to dry for several hours and then cover the bookmark with clear, adhesive covering film.

Parent's Handy Hint :-
Stamps can be removed from envelopes by soaking them in water. Dry the stamps on absorbent paper & press between books to keep them flat.

4cm. (1½")

23cm. (9")

4cm. (1½")

Jolly Joke Bookmark

What you need:-
An old joke book, or jokes cut out of comics.
A piece of cardboard.
Scissors.
A glue stick.

5cm. (2")

23cm. (9")

3cm. (1¼")

1. Cut the cardboard to measure 23cm x 5cm (9" x 2").

2. Measure 3cm (1¼") from the bottom of the strip, draw a line across it and make little snips up to the 3cm (1¼") line. This makes a frilly bottom edge for the bookmark.

3. Carefully cut out the jokes from the book or comics and glue them all over both sides of the bookmark, being sure each joke is kept whole and can be read. Leave a tiny space between each joke, so that the cardboard shows through.

Parent's Handy Hint:-
Use jokes appropriate to the person who will receive the present, e.g. Doctor jokes if the bookmark is to be given to a Doctor.

Where do frogs hang their coats? In the croakroom!

What goes croak dot, croak dot, croak dot? Morse toad!

What kind of shoes do frogs wear? Open toad!

What is green and lives in a lighthouse? A frog horn!

Handy Jotter

Parent's Handy Hints :-
Encourage your child to carry out the measuring & cutting involved in this project which will help develop skills of precision.

What you need :-

Stiff cardboard.
Wallpaper.   A punch.
Glue.   A ruler.
Paper.
Scissors.
A small piece of Velcro.
A small piece of ribbon or cord.

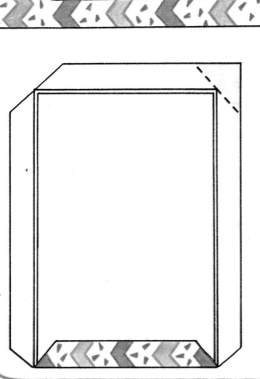

1. Take a piece of stiff cardboard approximately 20cm x 12cm (8″ x 4½″) and cover with wallpaper, cutting and glueing as shown.

2. Cut out a piece of paper slightly smaller than the cardboard and glue to the back.

3. Cut out twenty pieces of white paper approximately 11cm (4″) square from one large piece as shown opposite or use scrap paper.

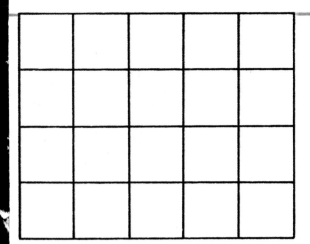

pencil and half to the jotter and attach the pencil. To hang the jotter, thread a piece of decorative ribbon, tape or cord through the hole.

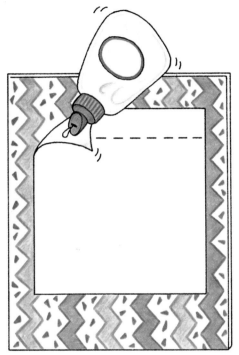

4. Take the first piece of paper and glue the top edge firmly to the front of the jotter leaving about 4cm (1½″) of wallpaper showing at the bottom.

5. Glue on each sheet to the one below in this way. Punch a hole through the top of the jotter.

6. Take a tiny pencil and 2cm (¾″) of Velcro. Glue half to the

The pencil could be covered in wallpaper to match the jotter.

Bird Mobile

What you need:-
Cardboard.
Pencil.
Crayons or paints.
Scissors.
A darning needle.
Crepe paper.
Thread.
Tissue paper.
Glue.

50cms (20")
45cm. (18")

BIRD SHAPE
Wing slot

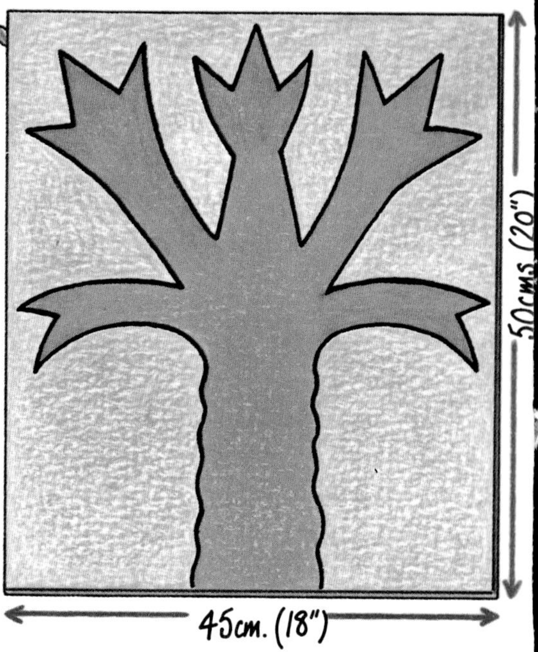

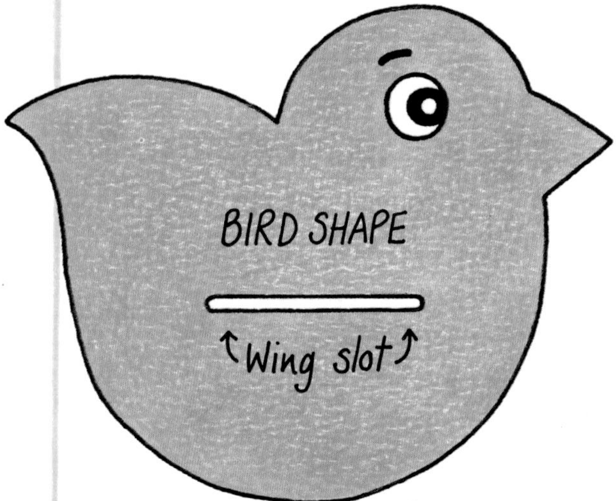

1. Take a piece of cardboard approximately 50cm x 45cm (20″ x 18″), draw on the tree shape and cut it out.

2. Crayon or paint both sides to look like a tree.

3. Cut out the basic shapes of four birds from cardboard and paint them.

4. Pleat four small pieces of crepe paper and make a slit with sharp pointed scissors through the middle of each bird's body.

Parent's Handy Hints:-
Help your child to make the wing slot with the scissors & the holes using the darning needle. Also, help to suspend the finished mobile from the ceiling.

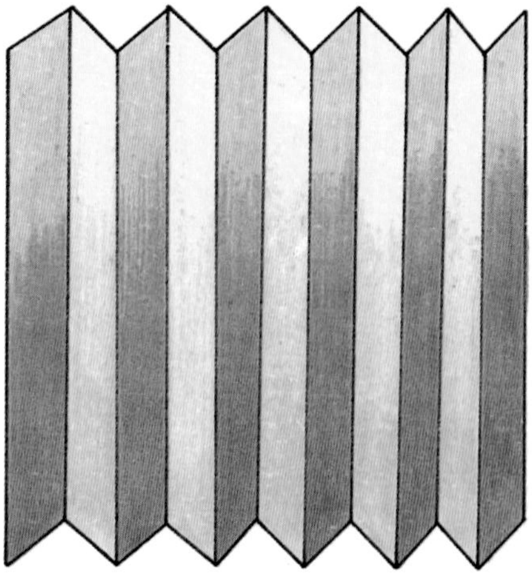

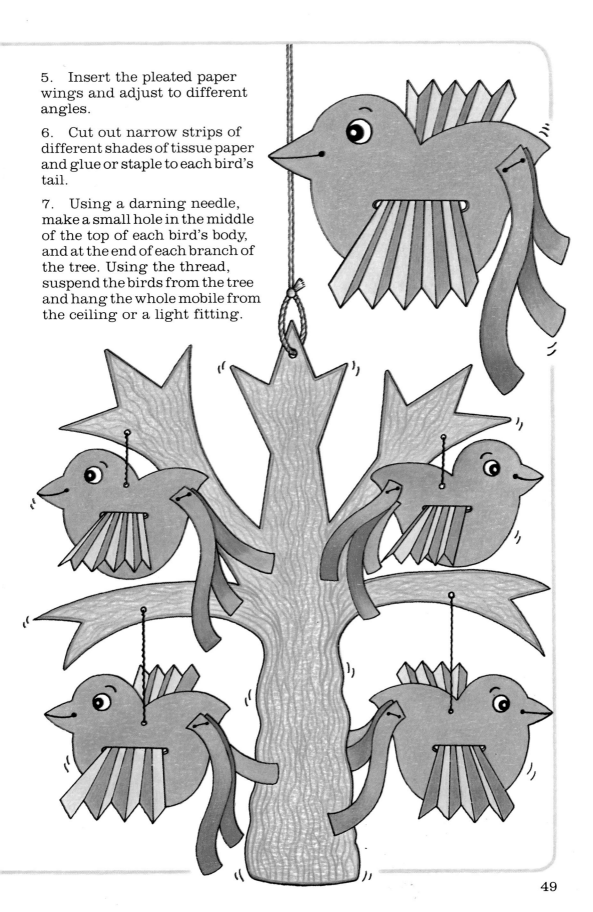

5. Insert the pleated paper wings and adjust to different angles.

6. Cut out narrow strips of different shades of tissue paper and glue or staple to each bird's tail.

7. Using a darning needle, make a small hole in the middle of the top of each bird's body, and at the end of each branch of the tree. Using the thread, suspend the birds from the tree and hang the whole mobile from the ceiling or a light fitting.

49

Pirate Pen Holder

What you need :-
A yogurt carton.
A sharp pencil.
Gummed paper.
Scissors.   Glue.
A pink tissue   Felt.
   Cotton wool.

Parent's Handy Hint :- Yogurt cartons must be thoroughly washed & dried before use!

1.   Wash and thoroughly dry a yogurt carton, and turn it upside down. With a sharp pencil make a hole through the bottom large enough to hold a pen. Now cover the carton with bright gummed paper.

2.   Cut out arm shapes as shown from the same paper and a belt from a contrasting shade of paper. Glue on the arms and belt.

3.   To make a head, take a pink tissue and wrap it around a ball of cotton wool and glue to secure. Glue this firmly to the bottom of the carton close to the front.

4.   Cut out the pirate's eye and eye patch, moustache and nose from the gummed paper and stick them on to the face.

5.   Cut out a pirate's hat from the felt and glue to the head.

6.   Place a pen in the hole.

Clown Pencil Holder

Parent's Handy Hint :-
Felt pens or crayons can be used instead of gummed paper to decorate your clown.

What you need :-
A toilet roll tube.
Gummed paper.
Scissors.   Glue.
Cardboard.   Wool.
Crayons or felt pens.
Tissue paper.

1. Take a toilet roll tube and cover it with gummed paper to make the body of the clown.

2. Cut out the feet from card and cover with gummed paper.

3. For the head, cut out a circle 10cm (4″) across from cardboard. Add eyes, nose and mouth from gummed paper shapes, or draw them on with a felt tipped pen.

4. Cut out a clown hat shape from card and cover with gummed paper and glue on strands of wool for hair. When dry, carefully glue the hat on to the top of the head.

5. Glue the head and the feet firmly to the body. Crumple up small pieces of tissue paper to make pom-poms. Glue them to the hat, and to the body for buttons.

6. Keep pencils in the tube.

51

Dad's Desk Set

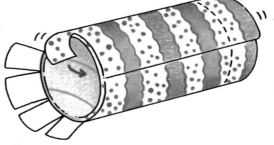

What you need :—
A piece of thick cardboard.
3 empty matchboxes.
1 empty cake mix box.
1 toilet roll tube.
3 brass paper fasteners.
A large piece of wrapping paper.
A pencil & a ruler.
Scissors. Glue.

The Letter-box

1. On the front of the cake mix box, draw a line 6cm (2½″) from the top. Then on each side draw a line from the front 6cm (2½″) line to the back top corner.

2. Cut off the top of the box along the lines.

3. Lay the box on wrapping paper and measure enough paper to wrap around the box, with 2cm (¾″) extra at the top and bottom.

4. Spread glue over the box and wrap the paper around it, folding at the bottom like the square gift shown on pages 12 and 13.

5. Snip the paper at each corner at the top of the box. Spread a little glue along the edge of the paper and fold over to finish off neatly.

Pen and Pencil Holder

1. Cut out a piece of wrapping paper wide enough to wrap around the toilet roll tube and to overlap by 1cm (½″), and deep enough to overlap by 2cm (¾″) at the top and bottom.

2. Spread glue on the outside of the tube and wrap the wrapping paper around the tube, leaving enough at the top and bottom to turn in.

3. Spread a little glue just inside the top and bottom of the tube. Snip the paper a few times to make it easier to turn it over and glue down inside the tube.

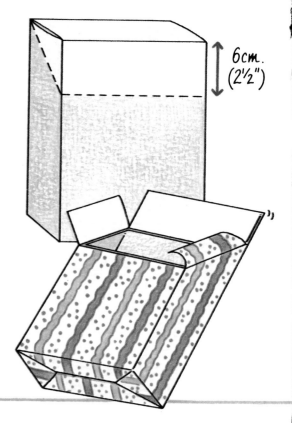

6cm.
(2½″)

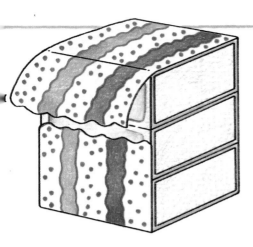

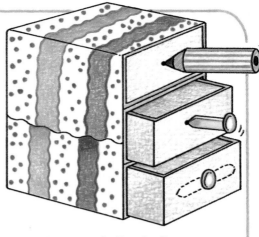

Paper Clip and Pin Drawers

1. Glue the three match boxes together on top of each other.

2. Cut out a strip of wrapping paper long enough to go all the way around the three match boxes.

3. Spread glue on the outside of the match boxes and wrap the paper carefully around them. Press down and leave to dry.

4. Make a small hole in the front of each drawer with a sharp pencil, then push a paper fastener through and flatten at the back.

Base for Dad's Desk Set

1. Now to put it all together. Spread glue down one side of the pen holder and the paper clip drawers. Attach them to either side of the letter-box and leave to dry.

2. Cut out a piece of thick cardboard wide enough to stand your desk tidy on with an extra 4cm (1¾″) at the front and back to make it sturdy. Cover with wrapping paper as shown on pages 12 and 13.

3. Spread glue on the bottom of the pen holder, letter-box and paper clip drawers and press down in the middle of the cardboard base.

Parent's Handy Hint :-
Pencils can also be covered to match! See p.57.

A Cook's Herb Garden

What you need :-
Several yogurt pots.
Compost.   A bowl.
Packets of herb seeds.
Ice lolly sticks.
A felt tipped pen.
A small tray.
A sharp pencil.
Model clay.
Cellophane.
Oil based paints & brush.

MODEL CLAY →

Parent's Handy Hint :-
This makes a useful present for a person who enjoys the cooking and will use the freshly grown herbs.

1.   Decorate the yogurt pots with bright paint.

2.   Carefully make several drainage holes at the bottom of each pot.

3.   Put the compost into a large bowl. Water it well. Take out a handful and squeeze the moisture out of it. Gently press it into the pot. Continue until all the pots are full.

4. Sprinkle the herbs into each pot and press them gently into the compost.

5. Write the name of each herb on an ice lolly stick then press the correct stick into each pot of herbs.

6. Put all the cartons on to the tray and cover it with cellophane.

PARSLEY

THYME

PARSLEY

SAGE

Pot Pourri

What you need :-

Rose petals, or any strongly scented petals. Cloves. Salt. A small wicker basket. Cellophane.

Adult's Handy Hints :-

Tell the person who receives this present to stir the petals round every other day, and to add new petals quite often.

1. Put the petals into a large bowl.

2. Sprinkle some salt over them and stir gently.

3. Next, sprinkle a handful of cloves over the petals and stir very gently.

4. Carefully put them all into a wicker basket.

5. Cover with cellophane or cling-film.

Pot Pourri Holder

What you need:-

A margarine tub.
Green crepe or tissue paper.
Scissors.
Glue. Ruler.
A pencil.

1. Cut out a piece of green paper long enough to go around the tub and wide enough to tuck over the top and underneath it.

2. Cut out a second piece of green paper, the same length as the first, but half as wide.

3. Wrap the larger piece of paper around the tub and glue the edges together at the join. Spread glue over the bottom of the tub and fold the paper underneath.

4. Spread a ring of glue just inside the rim of the tub. Turn the paper over, pressing firmly onto the glue.

5. Fold the second piece of paper in half three times. Draw a line 4cm (1½″) from the top and cut a zig-zag line from the top to the pencil line.

6. Unfold the paper and glue the straight edge inside the rim of the tub. Fold the zig-zag edge over to give a pretty finish.

A Needle Case

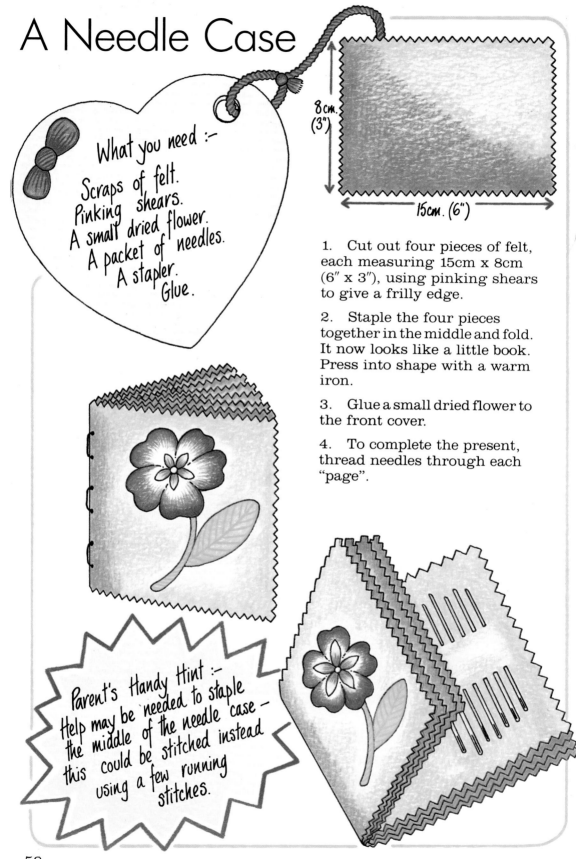

What you need :-

Scraps of felt.
Pinking shears.
A small dried flower.
A packet of needles.
A stapler.
Glue.

8cm. (3")

15cm. (6")

1. Cut out four pieces of felt, each measuring 15cm x 8cm (6" x 3"), using pinking shears to give a frilly edge.

2. Staple the four pieces together in the middle and fold. It now looks like a little book. Press into shape with a warm iron.

3. Glue a small dried flower to the front cover.

4. To complete the present, thread needles through each "page".

Parent's Handy Hint :-
Help may be needed to staple the middle of the needle case – this could be stitched instead using a few running stitches.

Heart Basket

What you need :-
Stiff cardboard.   Felt.
A pencil.   Glue.
Paint or crayons.
Gummed paper.
Sequins.
Lace.

Parent's Handy Hint :-
The heart basket can hold a small packet of sweets, a fancy handkerchief, a bottle of perfume or a lavender sachet.

1.   Take two pieces of stiff cardboard approximately 25cm x 20cm (10″ x 8″). Draw and cut out two matching heart shapes. Paint or crayon them.

2.   Glue the sides of the hearts together leaving the top open. When dry gently push the sides in to open the basket.

3.   Cut out a strip of felt 1cm x 45cm (½″ x 18″) in the same shade, or pleasantly contrasting, and glue to the top of the basket to make a handle.

4.   Cut out two smaller matching hearts from gummed paper and glue one to the front and one to the back of the basket.

5.   Glue lace along the top of the basket and sequins around the edge.

Egg Box Butterfly

1. Take a cardboard egg box and cut off the lid.

2. Cut the base in half longways to give three egg sections and paint these brightly.

3. Cut out a pair of wings from thin cardboard in the shape shown and paint or crayon them in a pattern of your choice.

What you need:—
A cardboard egg box.
Scissors.
Paint or crayons.
Thin cardboard.
Adhesive tape.
A pipe cleaner.
Felt tipped pens.

Wing pattern.

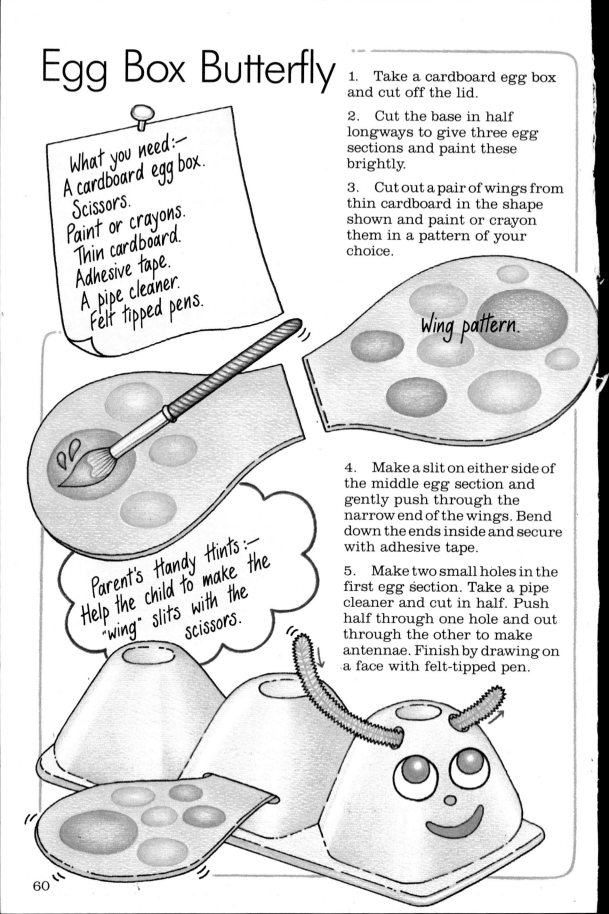

4. Make a slit on either side of the middle egg section and gently push through the narrow end of the wings. Bend down the ends inside and secure with adhesive tape.

5. Make two small holes in the first egg section. Take a pipe cleaner and cut in half. Push half through one hole and out through the other to make antennae. Finish by drawing on a face with felt-tipped pen.

Parent's Handy Hints:—
Help the child to make the "wing" slits with the scissors.

Egg Box Chicks

1. Take two polystyrene egg boxes. Carefully remove the fastening flap (keep to use later) and cut the lid in half longways. Staple the front three egg sections securely to the base.

2. Cut out beaks and feet from pieces of bright cardboard using the patterns shown here as a guide. Fold the beak in half.

What you need :-
2 polystyrene egg boxes.
Scissors.
Stapler.
Cardboard.
Plastic based glue.
Darning needle.
Feathers.

3. Make a small slit in the front of each egg section and insert the beaks.

4. Draw on eyes using a felt-tipped pen and glue the feet into place using a plastic-based glue.

5. Cut out the small raised pieces from the fastening flap and glue on to the chicks' heads. Using a darning needle pierce a hole in the back of each chick's head and insert a bright feather for the tail.

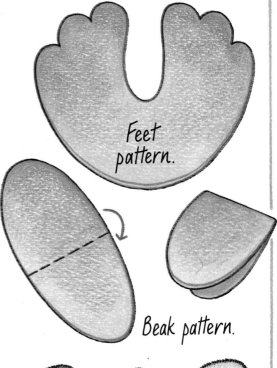

Feet pattern.

Beak pattern.

A Friendship Tree

1. Glue the white paper to the thick cardboard and leave to dry.

2. Draw a very large tree, with long branches and leaves, on the paper. When it looks good, paint the tree brown and the leaves green.

What you need :-
A large sheet of white paper.
A piece of stiff cardboard
(the same size as the paper).
Strong glue.
Paints.
A brush.
A pencil.
Photographs or pictures
of friends, pop singers,
T.V. stars or family.

Parent's Handy Hints :-
This is an absorbing project that can be adapted to suit any child's circumstances and could be used as a family tree. It makes a wonderful present for a close friend or member of the family.

Famous people.

T.V. STAR or POP SINGER

or CLOSE RELATION.

MAN YOU ADMIRE.

B
FR

BR